I0410875

Outlook E-mail Security in the Midst of Malicious Code Attacks

By: Trent Pitsenbarger and Paul Bartock

of the

Systems and Network Attack Center (SNAC)

W2Kguides@nsa.gov

Dated: 30 Dec. 2004
Version 3.1

Warnings

- **Do not attempt to implement any of the settings in this guide without first testing in a non-operational environment.**

- This document is only a guide containing recommended security settings. It is not meant to replace well-structured policy or sound judgment. Furthermore this guide does not address site-specific configuration issues. Care must be taken when implementing this guide to address local operational and policy concerns.

- SOFTWARE IS PROVIDED "AS IS" AND ANY EXPRESS OR IMPLIED WARRANTIES, INCLUDING, BUT NOT LIMITED TO, THE IMPLIED WARRANTIES OF MERCHANTABILITY AND FITNESS FOR A PARTICULAR PURPOSE ARE EXPRESSLY DISCLAIMED. IN NO EVENT SHALL THE CONTRIBUTORS BE LIABLE FOR ANY DIRECT, INDIRECT, INCIDENTAL, SPECIAL, EXEMPLARY, OR CONSEQUENTIAL DAMAGES (INCLUDING, BUT NOT LIMITED TO, PROCUREMENT OF SUBSTITUTE GOODS OR SERVICES; LOSS OF USE, DATA, OR PROFITS; OR BUSINESS INTERRUPTION) HOWEVER CAUSED AND ON ANY THEORY OF LIABILITY, WHETHER IN CONTRACT, STRICT LIABILITY, OR TORT (INCLUDING NEGLIGENCE OR OTHERWISE) ARISING IN ANY WAY OUT OF THE USE OF THIS SOFTWARE, EVEN IF ADVISED OF THE POSSIBILITY OF SUCH DAMAGE.

- Please keep track of the latest security patches and advisories at the Microsoft security bulletin page at http://www.microsoft.com/technet/security/current.asp.

- This document contains possible recommended settings for the system Registry. You can severely impair or disable a Windows System with incorrect changes or accidental deletions when using a Registry editor (Regedt32.exe or Regedit.exe) to change the system configuration. Currently, there is no "undo" command for deletions within the Registry. Registry editor prompts you to confirm the deletions if "Confirm on Delete" is selected from the options menu. When you delete a key, the message does not include the name of the key you are deleting. Therefore, check your selection carefully before proceeding.

Trademark Information

Microsoft, MS-DOS, Windows, Windows 2000, Windows XP, Windows NT, Windows 98, Windows 95, Windows for Workgroups, and Windows 3.1 are either registered trademarks or trademarks of Microsoft Corporation in the U.S.A. and other countries.

All other names are registered trademarks or trademarks of their respective companies.

Table of Contents

Introduction

E-mail based attacks, which reached a state of infamy with the ILOVEYOU worm and a host of more recent attacks, have highlighted the propensity of modern e-mail systems to provide a ready conduit for malicious code delivery. The Microsoft family of e-mail clients has proven to be a particularly attractive target for malicious code writers, primarily due to their widespread usage and their rich programming model.

The numerous e-mail based attacks that have hit the Internet over the last few years have taken varying approaches to compromising systems, but in general they have taken two basic forms. Some rely on the cooperation of the victim. An e-mail message with a malicious attachment may be disguised such that it appears to contain important or interesting information in an attempt to lure the victim into opening the attachment and thereby launching the attack. Others rely on known vulnerabilities within the client. Numerous attacks have taken advantage of security weaknesses that allow attachments or scripts embedded in the message to execute simply by virtue of previewing the message.

The remainder of this document presents a variety of countermeasures that can be applied to limit the vulnerability of e-mail systems to these kinds of attacks. It focuses primarily on the Microsoft Outlook clients, given the prominent role those applications played in recent incidents. Both the Outlook and Outlook Express clients are covered.

Most of these recommendations are taken from a series of configuration guides written by NSA's Systems and Network Attack Center (SNAC). Based upon informal surveys of SNAC customers, it appears that the impact of e-mail based attacks have been greatly minimized in organizations that followed these guidelines. For a complete set of our security configuration guides, visit our website at http://www.nsa.gov. Click on *About NSA/Information Assurance/Security Recommendation Guides*.

As always, these procedures should be vetted on a test LAN prior to their usage on an operational network. While the authors have positive experiences with each of these recommendations, it is impossible for our testing to fully emulate other operational environments.

Countermeasures:

The following are a set of specific countermeasures that can help reduce the threat caused by the various kinds of malicious payloads affecting Outlook clients.

Countermeasure 1 – Microsoft's E-mail Security Updates

Outlook 2000

As a direct result of the ILOVEYOU worm and other similar computer security incidents, Microsoft released a series of updates for Outlook 2000 to improve the application's security posture.

The first update, called the Outlook E-mail Attachment Security Update, prevents one from opening certain file types directly from an e-mail message. Instead, these file types must be copied to disk before they can be opened. This is intended to cause one to pause before opening an attachment of a type that is viewed as being particularly prone to abuse as a means of transferring malicious code. This patch is no longer available on Microsoft's web site. Links to this patch have been updated to point to Office 2000 Service Pack 3, which is discussed below.

The second update shipped with Microsoft Outlook SR-1. This update functions exactly like the first one, except the list of affected files can be modified via registry keys set on the client computer.

The third update, which is the recommended solution for Outlook 2000, is included with Office 2000 Service Pack 3. With this update, attachments that present the greatest threat – referred to as "Level 1" attachments in the Microsoft lexicon – are stripped from incoming messages and from all previously saved messages. The list of Level 1 file types is enumerated in the following table:

File extension	Level 1 File types
.ade	Microsoft Access Project Extension
.adp	Microsoft Access Project
.app	Microsoft Visual FoxPro Application, Executable Application
.bas	Visual Basic Class Module
.bat	Batch File
.chm	Compiled HTML Help File
.cmd	Windows Command Script
.com	MS-DOS Program
.cpl	Control Panel Extension
.crt	Security Certificate
.csh	Kornshell Script File
.exe	Program
.fxp	Microsoft Visual FoxPro Compiled Program
.hlp	Help File
.hta	HTML Program
.inf	Setup Information
.ins	Internet Communication Settings
.isp	Internet Service Provider Settings
.js	JScript Script File
.jse	JScript Encoded Script File
.ksh	Kornshell Script File
.lnk	Shortcut
.mda	Microsoft Access Add-In Program

File extension	Level 1 File types
.mdb	Microsoft Access Database
.mde	Microsoft Access MDE Database
.mdt	Microsoft Access Workgroup Information
.mdw	Microsoft Access Workgroup Information
.mdz	Microsoft Access Wizard Program
.msc	Microsoft Common Console Document
.msi	Windows Installer Package
.msp	Windows Installer Patch
.mst	Windows SDK Setup Transform Script
.ops	Office Profile Settings
.pcd	Visual Test Compiled Test Script
.pif	Shortcut To MS-DOS Program
.prf	Microsoft Outlook Profile Settings
.prg	Microsoft Visual FoxPro Program
.pst	Microsoft Outlook Personal Folders File
.reg	Registry Data File
.scf	Windows Explorer Command
.scr	Screen Saver
.sct	Windows Script Component
.shb	Shortcut Into A Document
.shs	Shell Scrap Object
.url	Internet Shortcut
.vb	Vbscript File
.vbe	Vbscript Encoded Script File
.vbs	Visual Basic Script File
.wsc	Windows Script Component
.wsf	Windows Script File
.wsh	Windows Scripting Host Settings

Table 1: Level 1 File Types, Outlook 2000 with Service Pack 3

Users will see a warning if they try to send an e-mail message that contains any Level 1 file attachment; however, the attachment is not actually stripped at the sender's end. If the receiving user is not running Outlook with an appropriate attachment security update, the attachment will be accessible.

If an Outlook 2000 user tries to forward a message containing a restricted file extension attachment, Outlook will strip the attachment from the forwarded copy before it is sent.

This update handles what is defined as "Level 2" attachments in a different manner. Level 2 attachments are not blocked, but instead the user is required to save them to the hard disk before executing. This is intended to cause the user to pause before acting and not just absent-mindedly launch a potentially malicious attachment. By default, no file types are included in Level 2; however, the administrator can define the files types that should be included in Level 2.

There are two ways that the Outlook 2000 SP3 file attachment behavior can be modified. The first method is strictly controlled by the administrator and requires the installation of an add-on to the Exchange Server. This add-on, called the Outlook Security Template, gives the administrator fine grain control over the definition of Level 1 and Level 2 file types and much more, but only for those users whose mail is delivered to an Exchange mail box (as opposed to a .pst file). This add-on is described in detail - including installation procedures - in the instructions accompanying the add-on and in Chapter 2 of the *Guide to the Secure Configuration and Administration of Microsoft Exchange 2000*. This document is available at http://www.nsa.gov and includes a number of additional security recommendations not detailed in this document.

End users can modify the list of Level 1 attachments via registry key settings only if the change is not prohibited as described below. The applicable settings are located under the key:

HKEY_CURRENT_USER\Software\Microsoft\Office\9.0\Outlook\Security

To remove a file from the Level 1 definition, navigate to this key and add a string value named *Level1Remove*. Set the value of this registry to specify the file types to be demoted as a semicolon delimited list, as in: .abc; .def. Use a *Level1Add* string value under this same key to promote file types to Level 1. These settings will take effect the next time Outlook 2000 is started.

Giving users this much flexibility is generally not a good idea from a security perspective. Administrators can prohibit users from demoting file types from Level 1 by using the Outlook Security Template (again, under the assumption that the user's mail is being delivered to an Exchange mail box). Users cannot remove any extensions that were explicitly added to the Level 1 list using the security template. For example, if user wants to remove .exe files from the Level 1 group, but that file extension had b added by the administrator in the Level 1 *Add* box, then the user would not be able to remove .exe files from the group[1].

Administrators can also prohibit demotions from Level 1 by setting a registry key within HKCU that regular users cannot modify. This would be particularly useful for those installations not running the Outlook Security Template. Create the following key and value name. Do not set a value; Outlook simply looks for the presence of the value name.

HKCU\Software\Policies\Microsoft\Office\9.0\Outlook
Value name: DisallowAttachmentCustomization

---

[1] The reader may notice that the Outlook Security Template has a feature entitled "Allow users to lower attachments to Level 2;" however, this feature is not supported in Outlook 2000 and therefore cannot be used to control a user's ability to downgrade file attachments.

A number of additional file related settings are controlled by the Outlook Security Template. Most notable are settings that can allow in-place activation of OLE packaged objects. These represent additional ways in which files can be included with an e-mail message and as such should not be enabled.

Finally, note that in addition to installing and configuring the Outlook Security Template, the client must be configured to use the template. This is accomplished by setting a DWORD registry key on the client to 1:

HKey_Current_User\Software\Policies\Microsoft\Security\CheckAdminSettings

In summary, it is recommended to run the Outlook Security Template where possible so that the administrator can have control of the attachment security settings from a convenient, centralized location. The administrator should explicitly list all prohibited attachment types in the Level 1 Add box to prevent users from demoting them or setting the DisallowAttachmentCustomization option.

Outlook 2002 and Outlook 2003

Outlook 2002 and Outlook 2003 are nearly identical in terms of this countermeasure and will be discussed concurrently. Minor differences between the two will be highlighted, the most noticeable of which relates to the registry keys that include the Microsoft Office version number in the path. In this document the versioning information is indicated with the variable [Version Number] which should be replaced with the following values:

For Outlook 2002/2003: 10.0
For Outlook 2003: 11.0

The e-mail security features available in Outlook 2002/2003 are very similar to those le in Outlook 2000 SP3. There are some notable differences in relation to the file types that are blocked by default and the options supported under the k Security Template that lead to a slightly different set of recommendations.

Outlook 2002/2003 supports the notion of Level 1 and Level 2 file types in the same manner as Outlook 2000; however, the specific file types defined as Level 1 have evolved in Outlook 2002 and Outlook 2003 and can even be dependent on the service pack being run. Table 1 reflects Outlook 2002 with Service Pack 3. Outlook 2003 blocks all these file types, plus those reflected in Table 3.

File extension	Level 1 File types
.ade	Microsoft Access Project Extension
.adp	Microsoft Access Project
.app	Microsoft Visual FoxPro Application, Executable Application
.bas	Visual Basic Class Module

File extension	Level 1 File types
.bat	Batch File
.cer	Certificate File
.chm	Compiled HTML Help File
.cmd	Windows Command Script
.com	MS-DOS Program
.cpl	Control Panel Extension
.crt	Security Certificate
.csh	Kornshell Script File
.exe	Program
.fxp	Microsoft Visual FoxPro Compiled Program
.hlp	Help File
.hta	HTML Program
.inf	Setup Information
.ins	Internet Communication Settings
.isp	Internet Service Provider Settings
.js	JScript Script File
.jse	JScript Encoded Script File
.ksh	Kornshell Script File
.lnk	Shortcut
.mda	Microsoft Access Add-In Program
.mdb	Microsoft Access Database
.mde	Microsoft Access MDE Database
.mdt	Microsoft Access Workgroup Information
.mdw	Microsoft Access Workgroup Information
.mdz	Microsoft Access Wizard Program
.msc	Microsoft Common Console Document
.msi	Windows Installer Package
.msp	Windows Installer Patch
.mst	Windows SDK Setup Transform Script
.ops	Office Profile Settings
.pcd	Visual Test Compiled Test Script
.pif	Shortcut To MS-DOS Program
.prf	Microsoft Outlook Profile Settings
.prg	Microsoft Visual FoxPro Program
.pst	Microsoft Outlook Personal Folders File
.reg	Registry Data File
.scf	Windows Explorer Command
.scr	Screen Saver
.sct	Windows Script Component
.shb	Shortcut Into A Document
.shs	Shell Scrap Object
.tmp	Temporary File

File extension	Level 1 File types
.url	Internet Shortcut
.vb	Vbscript File
.vbe	Vbscript Encoded Script File
.vbs	Visual Basic Script File
.vsmacros	Visual Studio .NET Binary Based Macro Project
.vss	Visio SmartShapes Image File
.vst	Visio Template File
.vsw	Visio Workspace File
.ws	Windows Script File
.wsc	Windows Script Component
.wsf	Windows Script File
.wsh	Windows Scripting Host Settings

Table 2: Level 1 File Types, Outlook 2002 with Service Pack 3

File extension	Level 1 File types
.asp	Active Server Page
.its	Internet Document Set, International Translation
.mad	Access Module Shortcut
.maf	Access Form Shortcut
.mag	Access Diagram Shortcut
.mam	Access Macro Shortcut
.maq	Access Query Shortcut
.mar	Access Report Shortcut
.mas	Access Stored Procedures
.mat	Access Table Shortcut
.mau	Media Attachment Unit
.mav	Access View Shortcut
.maw	Access Data Access Page

Table 3: *Additional* File Types Block by Outlook 2003

Users will see a warning if they try to send an e-mail message that contains any Level 1 file attachment; however, the attachment is not actually stripped at the sender's end. If the receiving user is not running a version of Outlook that supports attachment blocking, the attachment will be accessible.

If an Outlook 2002/2003 user tries to forward a message containing a restricted file extension attachment, Outlook will strip the attachment from the forwarded copy before it is sent.

Level 2 attachments are not blocked, but instead the user is required to save them to the hard disk before executing. This is intended to cause the user to pause before acting and not just absent-mindedly launch a potentially malicious attachment. By default, no file types are included in Level 2; however, the administrator can define the files types that should be included in Level 2.

There are two ways that the Outlook 2002/2003 file attachment behavior can be modified. The first manner is strictly controlled by the administrator and requires the installation of an add-on to the Exchange Server. This add-on, called the Outlook Security Template, gives the administrator fine grain control over the definition of Level 1 and Level 2 file types and much more, but only for those users whose mail is delivered to an Exchange mail box (as opposed to a .pst file). This add-on is described in detail - including installation procedures - in the instructions accompanying the add-on and in Chapter 2 of the *Guide to the Secure Configuration and Administration of Microsoft Exchange 2000*. This document is available at http://www.nsa.gov and includes a number of additional security recommendations not detailed in this document.

End users can modify the list of Level 1 attachments via registry key settings only if the change is not prohibited in the Outlook Security template as described below. The applicable settings are located under the key:

HKEY_CURRENT_USER\Software\Microsoft\Office**[Version Number]**\Outlook\Security

To remove a file from the Level 1 definition, navigate to this key and add a string value named *Level1Remove*. Set the value of this registry to specify the file types to be demoted as a semicolon delimited list, as in: .abc; .def. Use a *Level1Add* string value under this same key to promote file types to Level 1. These settings will take effect the next time Outlook 2002/2003 is started.

Giving users this much flexibility is generally not a good idea from a security perspective. Administrators can prohibit users from demoting file types from Level 1 by using the Outlook Security Template (again, under the assumption that the user's mail is being delivered to an Exchange mail box). Simply by accepting the default condition of disabling the option *Allow users to lower attachments to Level 2*, the administrator can prevent users from demoting file types. Alternately, as with Outlook 2000, users cannot remove any extensions that were explicitly added to the Level 1 list using the security template. For example, if the user wants to remove .exe files from the Level 1 group, but that file extension had been added by the administrator in the Level 1 *Add* box, then the user would not be able to remove .exe files from the group.

Administrators can also prohibit demotions from Level 1 by setting a registry key within HKCU that regular users cannot modify. This would be particularly useful for those installations not running the Outlook Security Template. Create the following DWORD key and value name. Do not set a value; Outlook simply looks for the presence of the value name.

HKCU\Software\Policies\Microsoft\Office**[Version Number]**\Outlook
Value name: DisallowAttachmentCustomization

A number of additional file related settings are controlled by the Outlook Security Template. Most notable are settings that control in-place activation of OLE packaged objects. These represent additional ways in which files can be included with an e-mail message and as such should not be enabled.

Finally, note that in addition to installing and configuring the Outlook Security Template the client must be configured to use the template. This is accomplished by setting a DWORD registry key on the client:

HKey_Current_User\Software\Policies\Microsoft\Security\CheckAdminSettings

The value of the key relates to the name of the public folder in which the Outlook Security Template was published (reference the installation instructions):

Key State	Description
No key or key set to anything but 0,1, or 2	Outlook uses default administrative settings.
Set to 0	Outlook uses default administrative settings.
Set to 1	Outlook looks for custom administrative settings in the Outlook Security Settings folder.
Set to 2	Outlook looks for custom administrative settings in the Outlook 10 Security Settings folder.

Table 2: Outlook Security Template Client Settings for Outlook 2002/2003

It is recommended to run the Outlook Security Template where possible so that the administrator can have control of the attachment security settings from a convenient, centralized location. The administrator should disable the *Allow users to lower attachments to Level 2* option or explicitly list all prohibited attachment types in the Level 1 Add box to prevent users from demoting them. If using the Outlook Security Template is not practical, setting the DisallowAttachmentCustomization option should be considered.

Outlook 2002/2003 also have a highly recommended security feature that will strip out html from incoming messages. This is to prevent html scripting attacks that have been known to take advantage of Windows vulnerabilities by a simple preview of a message. To enable this feature in Outlook 2002, create the following registry key:

Key: [HKEY_CURRENT_USER\Software\Microsoft\Office\10.0\Outlook\Options\Mail]
Value Name: ReadAsPlain
Data Type: REG_DWORD
Value: 1 [enable]
      0 [disable]

Outlook 2003 does not support this key. Instead, the option is exposed via *Tools/Options/Preferences*. Click on E-mail options and enable *Read all standard mail in plain text* and *Read all digitally signed mail in plain text*.

Outlook Express

Outlook Express prior to version 6.0 had no intrinsic protection against malicious code. Version 6.0 offers the option to *Warn me when other applications try to send as me*. This option, accessible via the Tools/Options/Security menu, is enabled by default and is only relevant when Outlook Express is configured as the default simple MAPI client (in other words, enabled as the default mail handler under the Tool/Options/General tab) and another program attempts to use simple MAPI to send messages. There is also an option under the Tools/Options/Security menu to *not allow attachments to be saved or opened that could potentially be a virus*. The behavior of this feature is dependent on which service pack is being run.

Under the gold (initial) release and Service Pack 1 release, this option will deny access to a wide variety of files as determined by the *Confirm open after download* setting for the file type. The *Confirm open after download* setting is accessible from Windows Explorer. In Windows NT select View/Options/File Types tab, highlight the file type of interest, and click *Edit*. In Windows 2000 and Windows XP, select Tools/Folder Options/File Types tab, highlight the file type of interest, and click on *Advanced*. This setting controls not only the behavior of Outlook Express but dictates whether or not files open automatically when downloaded.

The *Do not allow attachments to be saved or opened that could potentially be a virus* setting is pretty draconian - by default it will block most file types, yet loosening the *confirm open after download* setting is not desirable. If running Outlook Express the best bet from strictly a security perspective is to enable both of these features, but from an operational perspective it may be better to disable the file attachments setting and rely on the recommendations of *Countermeasure 7 – Anti-Virus Products and Perimeter Attachment Blocking*.

Outlook Express Service Pack 2, which presently only ships with Windows XP Service Pack 2, takes advantage of the new Attachment Manager feature. This feature handles file attachments based upon a characterization of the risk associated with the file type. As described in Microsoft knowledge base article 883260, the following file types are considered high risk:

.ade	.hlp	.mar	.mst	.vb
.adp	.hta	.mas	.ops	.vbe
.app	.inf	.mat	.pcd	.vbs
.asp	.ins	.mau	.pif	.vsmacros
.bas	.isp	.mav	.prf	.vss
.bat	.its	.maw	.prg	.vst
.cer	.js	.mda	.pst	.vsw
.chm	.jse	.mdb	.reg	.ws
.cmd	.ksh	.mde	.scf	.wsc
.com	.lnk	.mdt	.scr	.wsf
.cpl	.mad	.mdw	.sct	.wsh
.crt	.maf	.mdz	.shb	
.csh	.mag	.msc	.shs	
.exe	.mam	.msi	.tmp	
.fxp	.maq	.msp	.url	

Access to these file types is prohibited if received as an attachment via Outlook Express assuming the *Do not allow attachments to be saved or opened that could potentially be a virus* feature is enabled. This setting is accessible under Tools/Options/Security.

Medium Risk File Types

File types that are not defined as high risk or low risk are labeled as medium risk. When one attempts to download or open medium risk files that originated in the Internet zone or from the restricted sites zone a warning may be offered but the action is allowed.

Low-risk file types

The Attachment Manager labels the following file types as low risk as long as they remain associated with Notepad. If they are associated with another program the file types are no longer considered low risk but instead are designated medium risk.

.log
.text
.txt

Similarly, the Attachment Manager labels the following file types as low risk only when associated with the Microsoft Windows Picture and Fax Viewer; otherwise, they are treated as medium risk:

.bmp	.jpe
.dib	.jpeg
.emf	.png
.gif	.tif
.ico	.tiff
.jfif	.wmf
.jpg	

This characterization of risk levels, and other aspects of Attachment Manager Functionality, can also be controlled via Group Policy via:

> User Configuration\Administrative Templates\Windows Components\ Attachment Manager

In order to manipulate these settings one must use a computer running Windows XP Service Pack 2.

Finally, Outlook Express in Windows XP Service Pack 1 and 2 includes the option of reading all messages in plain text format. This feature is available under Tools/Options/Read and is highly recommended to thwart delivery of html messages which are proven as an easy conduit for launching attacks.

Countermeasure 2 – Use of Internet Explorer Security Zones

Outlook and Outlook Express clients can take advantage of Internet Explorer security zones to protect against malicious code (ActiveX controls, Java, or scripts) embedded into the body of messages. Internet Explorer includes a capability to restrict the execution of such code based upon four zones. Before jumping into how Outlook uses these settings, a quick review of their use in Internet Explorer is in order.

- ☐ Local Intranet zone: This zone contains addresses that are typically behind the organization's firewall or proxy server. The default security level for the Local Intranet zone is "medium-low".
- ☐ Trusted Sites zone: This zone contains sites that are trusted -- sites that are believed not to contain files that could corrupt the computer or its data. The default security level for the Trusted Sites zone is "low".
- ☐ Restricted Sites zone: This zone contains sites that are not trusted -- that is, sites that may contain content that, if downloaded or run, could damage the computer or its data. The default security level for the Restricted Sites zone is "high".
- ☐ Internet zone: By default, this zone contains anything that is not on the computer or an intranet, or assigned to any other zone. The default security level for the Internet zone is "medium".

A plethora of security related settings can be configured for each of these zones. Microsoft has canned policies defined as *low*, *medium-low, medium*, and *high*, which the user can select, or alternately the user can tailor the settings to his or her specific needs.

Outlook utilizes these zones in that the user can select which of two zones -- the Internet zone or the Restricted zone -- Outlook messages fall into. The settings for the selected zone are then applied by Outlook to all messages. It is recommended to configure Outlook to use the "Restricted" zone. Outlook 2002/2003, Outlook 2000 with Service Pack 3, and Outlook Express 6.0 utilize this setting by default; however, prior versions do not. The setting is accessible by selecting Tools/Options and the Security tab.

The default settings for the Restricted zone are generally very conservative from a security perspective; however, a few variations from the default are recommended as detailed below. The specific settings available vary slightly depending on the version of Internet Explorer - not all of these settings will be available in all versions of Internet Explorer.

Run components not signed with Authenticode	**DISABLE**
Run components signed with Authenticode	**DISABLE**
Automatic prompting for ActiveX controls	**DISABLE**
Binary and script behaviors	**DISABLE**
Download signed ActiveX controls	**DISABLE**
Download unsigned ActiveX controls	**DISABLE**
Initialize and script ActiveX controls not marked as safe	**DISABLE**
Run ActiveX controls and plug-ins	**DISABLE**
Script ActiveX controls marked safe for scripting	**DISABLE**
Allow cookies that are stored on your computer	**DISABLE**
Allow per-session cookies (not stored)	**DISABLE**
File download	**DISABLE**
Font download	**DISABLE**
Java permissions	**DISABLE JAVA**
Access data sources across domains	**DISABLE**
Allow META REFRESH	**DISABLE**
Allow scripting of Internet Explorer web browser control	**DISABLE**
Allow script-initiated windows without size or position constraints	**DISABLE**
Allow Web pages to use restricted protocols for active content	**DISABLE**
Display mixed content	**DISABLE**
Don't prompt for client certificate selection when no certificates or only one certificate exists	**DISABLE**
Drag and drop or copy and paste files	**DISABLE**
Installation of desktop items	**DISABLE**
Launching programs within an IFRAME	**DISABLE**
Navigate sub-frames across different domains	**DISABLE**
Open files based on content, not file extension	**DISABLE**
Software channel permissions	**HIGH SAFETY**
Submit non-encrypted form data	**DISABLE**
Use Pop-up blocker	**ENABLED**
Userdata persistence	**DISABLE**
Web sites in low privileged web content zone can navigate into this zone	**DISABLE**
Active Scripting	**DISABLE**
Allow paste operations via script	**DISABLE**
Scripting of Java Applets	**DISABLE**
Logon	**Anonymous logon**

Note that following these recommendations will disable many advanced features; however, for the vast majority of e-mail users there will be no operational impact. This is because most e-mail messages are simple text messages with attachments. The features that are disabled deal primarily with script and controls embedded within the body of the message, which are not important to typical e-mail users. On the other hand, it is important to acknowledge that these settings are shared with the Internet Explorer browser, and web pages typically DO incorporate the kinds of features that are disabled via these settings. While this could represent an operational impact, keep in mind that the Restricted zone is intended to include those sites that are not trusted - one should restrict what those sites can do and in fact these recommended settings are only slightly more restrictive than the default settings for this zone.

These settings will counter many, but not all, known attacks that use active content contained within the body of e-mail messages and thus should not be considered an equivalent substitute to reading messages as plain text as recommended earlier.

Countermeasure 3 – Changing File Associations or Disabling WSH

Scripts that are executed by the Windows Scripting Host (WSH) have, at times, been a popular means of spreading malicious code. Running the latest versions of Outlook 2000, Outlook 2002/2003, and Outlook Express can provide users with protection against this form of attack as they can block access to these file types. If an organization is not running these latest versions, or has an operational need to allow WSH scripts to travel via e-mail, a level of protection can be achieved by changing the default action associated with the files. This will affect what occurs when a user launches (e.g., double-clicks) the script file.

The default action is changed via Windows Explorer. In Windows NT, select View/Options and the File Types tab, select the *VBScript Script File* entry, click *Edit*, highlight *Edit* in the *Actions* window, and click *Set Default*. With these changes invoked, if a user launches a .vbs attachment it will not be executed by the Windows Scripting Host. Instead, it will harmlessly open in the default editor (typically Notepad). Similarly, in Windows 2000 and Windows XP the default action associated with WSH scripts can be changed by selecting Tools/Folder Options and the File Types tab. Highlight the *VBS VBScript Script File* entry, click *Change,* and select *Notepad*.

This action should be completed not just for .vbs files but also for all code types interpretable by the Windows Scripting Host. The following file types are related to the Windows Scripting Host with only the .wsc and .sct extensions utilizing Notepad by default. Each should be set so that they open under Notepad.

- ☐ WSC
- ☐ WSH
- ☐ WSF
- ☐ SCT
- ☐ VBS
- ☐ VBE
- ☐ JS
- ☐ JSE

In addition, there are third party extensions available for the Windows Scripting Host that allow it to interpret other forms of code such as Perl or TCL. The default action for any third party extensions should be changed as well.

If dealing with Windows operating systems prior to Windows 2000 and clients other than Outlook or Outlook Express, it is important to note that the behavior may differ from what is represented here. For example, with some Netscape Messenger releases, if a user attempts to open an attachment he is presented with a choice to either open or save the attachment. If the user selects open, the code will be executed regardless of these settings. A second option for dealing with script attachments - disabling the Windows Scripting Host - will solve this problem.

Disabling the Windows Scripting Host is fairly easy to do: simply rename the core Windows programs that support script execution (wscript.exe and cscript.exe). These files reside in the %systemroot%\system32 directory (typically c:\winnt\system32 or c:\windows\system32). Note that renaming the files is a little tricky due to the protection Windows 2000/XP provides core files. It is necessary to first rename them in %SystemRoot%\system32\dllcache and then rename them in %SystemRoot%\system32. Cancel the "Windows File Protection" dialog box when it appears[2].

Finally, another option for disabling the Windows Scripting Host is to change the file permissions on cscript.exe and wscript.exe. This may be the preferred option if it is desired, for example, to allow administrators access while denying general users the ability to execute scripts.

It is important to note that countermeasure three should never be relied upon as the sole malicious code countermeasure. While it is effective against attacks that use these script files as their attack vector, it cannot possibly eliminate all risk, as there are other file types that could contain malicious code as well. A simple example to illustrate this point is .exe files – they are obviously critical to the operation of a PC and cannot be disabled, yet could easily be used as a malicious code delivery mechanism.

---

[2] If dealing with Windows operating systems prior to Windows 2000, it is best to do this from the command line or from a batch file. If the name is changed from Windows Explorer, some versions of the Windows operating system will automatically update file associations to reflect the new name – which, of course, renders the change ineffective.

Countermeasure 4 – MS Office Macro Protection and User Education

Microsoft provides for protection against some malicious file attachments through the associated application. For example, even though by default the e-mail security features of Countermeasure 1 do not address malicious Word macros, the Microsoft Office 2000, Office XP, and Office 2003 suites offer optional macro protection mechanisms that can help counter the threat in that they can be configured to only run macros that have been digitally signed by a trusted entity. In Word, PowerPoint, and Excel these options are accessible via *Tools/Macro/Security*. Select *High* (or *Very High* in the case of Office 2003) for maximum protection.

Countermeasure 5 – Displaying File Extensions

A common technique used to disguise malicious code is to make an executable appear as an innocuous file type. One way of doing this is to simply name the file with a superfluous file extension such as:

ILOVEYOU.TXT.VBS

If Windows is not configured to display file extensions, then this file, when viewed from Windows Explorer, would appear as a simple text file, as in:

ILOVEYOU.TXT

In order to preclude this kind of masquerading, two actions must be taken. First, set Windows to display file extensions via Windows Explorer. In Windows NT, select View/Options/View and disable (clear the check box) *Hide file extensions for known file types*. In Windows 2000 and Windows XP this setting is accessible by selecting Tools/Folder Options/View. Unfortunately, for certain file types that can contain or point to executable components, this setting has no effect. To configure Windows to display these file extensions, delete the registry keys listed in Table 3. Note that the presence of some of the keys are dependent on the operating system and applications installed - to ensure that all the applicable registry keys have been deleted for a given configuration, simply use regedit to search the registry for the string *NeverShowExt*.

File Extension	Registry Key	Notes
.cnf	HKEY_CLASSES_ROOT\ConferenceLink\NeverShowExt	NetMeeting's SpeedDial Object
.DeskLink	HKEY_CLASSES_ROOT\CLSID\{9E56BE61-C50F-11CF-9A2C-00A0C90A90CE}\NeverShowExt	Drag objects onto this folder to create a shortcut on the desktop
.lnk	HKEY_CLASSES_ROOT\lnkfile\NeverShowExt	Shortcut
.MAPIMail	HKEY_CLASSES_ROOT\CLSID\{9E56BE60-C50F-11CF-9A2C-00A0C90A90CE}\NeverShowExt	Drag objects onto this folder to mail them
.mydocs	HKEY_CLASSES_ROOT\CLSID\{ECF03A32-103D-11d2-854D-006008059367}\NeverShowExt	Drag objects onto this folder to create a copy in My Documents
.pif	HKEY_CLASSES_ROOT\piffile\NeverShowExt	Program information file (shortcut to a DOS program)
.scf	HKEY_CLASSES_ROOT\SHCmdFile\NeverShowExt	Explorer Command file
.shb	HKEY_CLASSES_ROOT\DocShortcut\NeverShowExt	Shortcut into a document
.shs	HKEY_CLASSES_ROOT\ShellScrap\NeverShowExt	Shell Scrap Object
.xnk	HKEY_CLASSES_ROOT\xnkfile\NeverShowExt	Shortcut to an Exchange folder
.url	HKEY_CLASSES_ROOT\InternetShortcut\NeverShowExt	Internet shortcut
.maw	HKEY_CLASSES_ROOT\Access.Shortcut.DataAccessPage.1\NeverShowExt	These extensions represent a series of shortcuts to elements of an MS Access database. Most components of an Access database can contain an executable component.
.mag	HKEY_CLASSES_ROOT\Access.Shortcut.Diagram.1\NeverShowExt	
.maf	HKEY_CLASSES_ROOT\Access.Shortcut.Form.1\NeverShowExt	
.mam	HKEY_CLASSES_ROOT\Access.Shortcut.Macro.1\NeverShowExt	
.mad	HKEY_CLASSES_ROOT\Access.Shortcut.Module.1\NeverShowExt	
.maq	HKEY_CLASSES_ROOT\Access.Shortcut.Query.1\NeverShowExt	
.mar	HKEY_CLASSES_ROOT\Access.Shortcut.Report.1\NeverShowExt	
.mas	HKEY_CLASSES_ROOT\Access.Shortcut.StoredProcedure.1\NeverShowExt	
.mat	HKEY_CLASSES_ROOT\Access.Shortcut.Table.1\NeverShowExt	
.mau	HKEY_CLASSES_ROOT\Access.Shortcut.Function.1\NeverShowExt	
.mav	HKEY_CLASSES_ROOT\Access.Shortcut.View.1\NeverShowExt	
.ZFSendTo Target	HKEY_CLASSES_ROOT\CLSID\{888DCA60-FC0A-11CF-8F0F-00C04FD7D062}\NeverShowExt (not found in Windows 2K)	Drag objects onto this folder to create a compressed copy

Table 3: "NeverShowExt" Registry Keys

Countermeasure 6 – Keeping Up-to-Date with Patches

Installing patches in a timely matter is critical. A variety of e-mail borne attacks such as Bubbleboy, BadTrans, Klez, and others have utilized vulnerabilities for which Microsoft had already released a patch.

Countermeasure 7 – Anti-Virus Products and Perimeter Attachment Blocking

Scanning for malicious code at both the perimeter and desktop is recommended. Most virus scanning products function by scanning for known malicious code signatures; therefore, they are ineffective against new or uncharacterized attacks. They can, however, be effective at preventing reoccurrences of past attacks. Some products also allow the definition of attachment types that are then blocked from entry onto the network - a "black list." Populating the black list can be problematic in that determining all the attachment types that represent unacceptable risk is a difficult problem given the plethora of file types. To assist with such an effort, Addendum A offers the list of file types that can be used as a starting point; however, it can be much easier, and potentially more secure, to utilize products that enforce the acceptance of only those attachment types allowed by the organization's security policy -- a "white list." A combination of both techniques is attractive as well. Assume that a hypothetical file extension .xyz is allowed via the organization's security policy but a known attack uses a file attachment entitled "open_me_please.xyz". Placing the .xyz file extension on the white list but blocking that specific file with a black list entry would be effective in this instance.

Countermeasure 8 – Respecting the Concept of Least Privilege

Least privilege is a basic tenet of computer security that basically means giving a user only those rights that s/he needs to do their job. Malicious code runs in the security context in which it was launched - practically speaking, this means in the context of the user launching the code. Good practices include making certain that administrative accounts are kept to a minimum, that administrators use a regular account as much as possible instead of logging in as administrator to do routine things such as reading their mail, and setting resource permissions properly.

Countermeasure 9 – Operating System Security

Protection against malicious code can be greatly improved by secure configuration of the underlying operating system. The recommended guidelines for operating system security are contained in the series of Windows NT, Windows 2000, and Windows XP security guides described in the introduction. It is recommended to consider these guidelines in their entirety, but from the standpoint of malicious code containment there are three distinct sets of recommendations that will be highlighted here - protecting critical elements of the System Registry, eliminating a known privilege elevation attack, and restricting access to Windows system directories.

Countermeasure 9a – Securing the System Registry

Malicious code frequently takes advantage of the weak permissions on critical registry keys such the RUN key, which is used to a launch executables each time the system is started. In Windows NT the default access permissions associated with many of these keys allow a user to CREATE or MODIFY the contents which offers malicious code a ready exploitation path. The Windows NT Registry key permissions should be set per the following recommendations. The security templates provided as part of the Windows NT guide referenced above incorporates these recommendations.

Registry Key	User Group	Permissions
\MACHINE\SOFTWARE\Microsoft\Windows *key and subkeys* Parameters used by the Win32 subsystem.	Administrators Authenticated Users CREATOR OWNER SYSTEM	Full Control Query Value, Set Value, Create Subkey, Enumerate Subkeys, Notify, Read Control Full Control Full Control
\MACHINE\SOFTWARE\Microsoft\Windows\ CurrentVersion\Run *key and subkeys* Contains names of executables to be run each time the system is started.	Administrators Authenticated Users SYSTEM	Full Control Read Full Control
\MACHINE\SOFTWARE\Microsoft\Windows\ CurrentVersion\RunOnce *key and subkeys* Contains the name of a program to be executed the first time a user ever logs on.	Administrators Authenticated Users SYSTEM	Full Control Read Full Control
\MACHINE\SOFTWARE\Microsoft\Windows\ CurrentVersion\RunOnceEx *key and subkeys* Contains setup information for some system components and Internet Explorer. Works much the same way as the RunOnce key.	Administrators Authenticated Users SYSTEM	Full Control Read Full Control
\MACHINE\SOFTWARE\Microsoft\Windows\ CurrentVersion\Shell Extensions *key and subkeys* Contains all shell extension settings, which are used to extend and expand the Windows NT interface.	Administrators Authenticated Users CREATOR OWNER SYSTEM	Full Control Read Full Control Full Control

Table 4: Windows NT Registry Keys and Permissions of Interest

In Windows 2000 and Windows XP, the default security permissions on these keys have been greatly tightened such that only Power Users and Administrators can write to these keys. The NSA security templates for these operating systems further restrict access to those keys as detailed below:

Registry Key	User Group	Permissions	Applies To
\MACHINE\SOFTWARE\Microsoft\ Windows Parameters used by the Win32 subsystem.	Administrators CREATOR OWNER SYSTEM Users	Full Control Full Control Full Control Read	This key and subkeys Subkeys only This key and subkeys This key and subkeys
\MACHINE\SOFTWARE\Microsoft\ Windows\CurrentVersion\Run Contains names of executables to be run each time the system is started.	Administrators CREATOR OWNER SYSTEM Users	Full Control Full Control Full Control Read	This key and subkeys Subkeys only This key and subkeys This key and subkeys
\MACHINE\SOFTWARE\Microsoft\ Windows\CurrentVersion\ RunOnce Contains the name of a program to be executed the first time a user ever logs on.	Administrators CREATOR OWNER SYSTEM Users	Full Control Full Control Full Control Read	This key and subkeys Subkeys only This key and subkeys This key and subkeys
\MACHINE\SOFTWARE\Microsoft\ Windows\CurrentVersion\ RunOnceEx Contains setup information for some system components and Internet Explorer. Works much the same way as the RunOnce key.	Administrators CREATOR OWNER SYSTEM Users	Full Control Full Control Full Control Read	This key and subkeys Subkeys only This key and subkeys This key and subkeys
\MACHINE\SOFTWARE\Microsoft\ Windows\CurrentVersion\ Shell Extensions Contains all shell extension settings, which are used to extend and expand the Windows NT interface.	Administrators CREATOR OWNER SYSTEM Users	Full Control Full Control Full Control Read	This key and subkeys Subkeys only This key and subkeys This key and subkeys

Table 5: Windows 2000 and Windows XP Registry Keys of Interest

Countermeasure 9b – Securing Additional Base Named Objects

Securing base objects within Windows NT prevents malicious code from gaining local administrator privileges by way of a dynamic-link library (DLL). Without this heightened security, malicious code could load into memory a file with the same name as a system DLL and redirect programs to it. Use the Registry Editor to create and set the value of the following registry key. This setting does not apply to Windows 2000 or Windows XP:

Hive: HKEY_LOCAL_MACHINE

Key: \System\CurrentControlSet\Control\Session Manager

Name: AdditionalBaseNamedObjectsProtectionMode

Type: REG_DWORD

Value: 1

Countermeasure 9c – Securing the System Directories

Some malicious code writes to the system directories as a part of its infection mechanism. Windows NT is particularly vulnerable given the permissive access control lists applied to these directories by default. The following permissions are recommended. Once again these settings are integral to the aforementioned NSA security configuration guides.

FOLDER OR FILE	USER GROUPS	RECOMMENDED PERMISSIONS	APPLIES TO
%WINNT% Contains many operating system executable programs.	Administrators Authenticated Users Authenticated Users CREATOR OWNER SYSTEM	Full Control Read, Write & Execute Read & Execute Full Control Full Control	This folder, subfolders, and files This folder only Subfolders and files only This folder, subfolders, and files This folder, subfolders, and files
%WINNT/SYSTEM Contains many operating system DLLs, drivers, and executable programs.	Administrators Authenticated Users CREATOR OWNER SYSTEM	Full Control Read & Execute Full Control Full Control	This folder, subfolders, and files This folder, subfolders, and files Subfolders and files only This folder, subfolders, and files
%WINNT/SYSTEM32 Contains many operating system DLLs, drivers, and executable programs (32 bit. Programs)	Administrators Authenticated Users CREATOR OWNER SYSTEM	Full Control Read, Execute Full Control Full Control	This folder, subfolders, and files This folder, subfolders, and files This folder, subfolders, and files This folder, subfolders, and files

Table 6: Windows NT Directories of Interest

Windows 2000 and Windows XP are better configured out-of-the-box to thwart this form of attack since, by default, users do not have write access to these directories. Nonetheless, applying the NSA security guidance is recommended as it will implement a slightly more conservative set of permissions on key directories as detailed below:

FOLDER OR FILE	USER GROUPS	RECOMMENDED PERMISSIONS	APPLIES TO
%SystemRoot% Contains many operating system executable programs.	Administrators CREATOR OWNER SYSTEM Users	Full Control Full Control Full Control Read & Execute	This folder, subfolders, and files Subfolders and files only This folder, subfolders, and files This folder, subfolders, and files
%SystemRoot%/SYSTEM Contains many operating system DLLs, drivers, and executable programs.	Administrators CREATOR OWNER SYSTEM Users	Full Control Full Control Full Control Read & Execute	This folder, subfolders, and files Subfolders and files only This folder, subfolders, and files This folder, subfolders, and files
%systemroot%/SYSTEM32 Contains many operating system DLLs, drivers, and executable programs (32 bit. Programs)	Administrators CREATOR OWNER SYSTEM Users	Full Control Full Control Full Control Read & Execute	This folder, subfolders, and files Subfolders and files only This folder, subfolders, and files This folder, subfolders, and files

Table 7: Windows 2000 and XP Directories of Interest

Final Word

Outlook has proven problematic from a malicious code standpoint given its rich programming model and widespread usage, but proper configuration can greatly reduce the risk. These countermeasures should be considered in the broader context of network security. Once again, the reader is directed to the NSA web site at http://www.nsa.gov, where a host of configuration guidance is provided that has proven very useful in improving the overall security posture of networks. Click on *Security Recommendation Guides* to access the suite of documents.

Addendum A - Candidate File Types for Inclusion in Blacklist

Creating a comprehensive black list of file types that could represent malicious code is a very difficult task given the overwhelming number of file extensions - this is why Countermeasure 7 suggests use of a white list when possible. Nonetheless, the following is a listing of file types that could serve as a conduit for malicious code that the reader may choose to use as an element of an organization's file blocking policy. In compiling this list, the following file types were included:

- system files
- executables
- script files that represent a common threat -- scripts associated with seldom used interpreters were not included
- document files which include an executable component and for which the associated application does not provide intrinsic mechanisms to reduce the risk of a malicious code attack
- configuration files

This list should only be used after careful consideration of the specific environment. It may be necessary to relax this recommendation in light of operational needs and it may be prudent to expand it. For instance, some organizations may elect to block .mp3 files given a lack of operational need and the common usage of this file type as a conduit for sharing bandwidth-hogging music files.

Analysis of additional file types is ongoing and, consequentially, the list may be modified from time-to-time.

Extension	Description
.386	Windows Enhanced Mode Driver or Swap File
.acm	Audio Compression Manager Driver and Windows System File
.ade	Microsoft Access Project Extension
.adp	Microsoft Access Project
.app	Microsoft Visual FoxPro Application, Executable Application
.asp	Active Server Page
.avb	Inoculan Anti-Virus Virus Infected File
.bas	Visual Basic Class Module
.bat	Batch File
.bin	BINARY FILE
.btm	4DOS Batch File
.cer	Certificate File
.chm	Compiled HTML Help File
.cla	Java Class File
.class	Java Class File

Extension	Description
.cmd	Windows Command Script
.cnv	MS Word Data Conversion File
.com	MS-DOS Program
.cpl	Control Panel Extension
.crt	Security Certificate
.cs*	Corel Script
.csh	Kornshell Script File
.dll	Dynamic Link Library
.drv	Device Driver
.exe	Program
.fon	Font
.fot	Font
.fxp	Microsoft Visual FoxPro Compiled Program
.hlp	Help File
.ht	HyperTerminal Session File
.hta	HTML Program
.htm*	Hypertext Markup Language
.htt	Hypertext Template
.inf	Setup Information
.ini	Initialization file
.ins	Internet Communication Settings
.isp	Internet Service Provider Settings
.its	Internet Document Set, International Translation
.js	JScript Script File
.jse	JScript Encoded Script File
.ksh	Kornshell Script File
.lib	Library File
.lnk	Shortcut
.mad	Access Module Shortcut
.maf	Access Form Shortcut
.mag	Access Diagram Shortcut
.mam	Access Macro Shortcut
.maq	Access Query Shortcut
.mar	Access Report Shortcut
.mas	Access Stored Procedures
.mat	Access Table Shortcut
.mau	Media Attachment Unit
.mav	Access View Shortcut
.maw	Access Data Access Page
.mda	Microsoft Access Add-In Program
.mdb	Microsoft Access Database
.mde	Microsoft Access MDE Database
.mdt	Microsoft Access Workgroup Information

Extension	Description
.mdw	Microsoft Access Workgroup Information
.mdz	Microsoft Access Wizard Program
.mht*	Archived Web Page
.mpd	Miniport Driver
.mrc	mIRC Script File
.msc	Microsoft Common Console Document
.msi	Windows Installer Package
.msp	Windows Installer Patch
.mst	Windows SDK Setup Transform Script
.ocx	Object Linking and Embedding (OLE) Control Extension
.ops	Office Profile Settings
.ov*	Program Overlay File
.pcd	Visual Test Compiled Test Scripts
.pci	Windows PCI Miniport file
.pdr	Port Driver
.perl	Perl Script
.pif	Program Information File
.pl	Perl Script
.plx	Executable Perl Script
.pm	Perl Module
.pnf	Precompiled Windows Setup Information
.prc	Palmpilot Resource File
.prf	Microsoft Outlook Profile Settings
.prg	Microsoft Visual FoxPro Program
.ps	Postscript
.pst	Microsoft Outlook Personal Folders File
.py	Python Script
.reg	Registry Data File
.rexx	Rexx Script
.rpm	RPM Package Manager
.scf	Windows Explorer Command
.scr	Screen Saver
.sct	Windows Script Component
.sh	Shell Script
.shb	Shortcut Into A Document
.shs	Shell Scrap Object
.smm	Ami Pro Macro
.so	Unix Shared Library
.sys	System Device Driver
.tcl	TCL/TK Language Script
.tlb	Type Library
.tmp	Temporary File
.tsp	Windows Telephony Service Provider

Extension	Description
.url	Internet Shortcut
.v*d	Virtual Device Driver
.vb	VBScript File
.vbe	VBScript Encoded Script File
.vbs	Visual Basic Script File
.vsmacros	Visual Studio .NET Binary Based Macro Project
.vss	Visio SmartShapes Image File
.vst	Visio Template File
.vsw	Visio Workspace File
.vxd	Virtual Device Driver
.wbt	WinBatch Script
.wch	PerfectScript Macro
.wcm	PerfectScript Macro
.wiz	Wizard File System Device Driver
.wml	Wireless Markup Language
.wmz	Windows Media Compressed Skin
.ws	Windows Script File
.wsc	Windows Script Component
.wsf	Windows Script File
.wsh	Windows Scripting Host Settings
.wsz	WinAmp Skin
.xpi	Browser Extension Archive
.xul	XML User Interface Language

Changes

Version 1.1 –
- ☐ Added detail concerning the ability of the Microsoft Office 2000 suite to limit macro execution to those that have been signed by a trusted entity.
- ☐ Detailed how *regedit.exe* can be used with an undocumented */s* option to suppress message boxes.
- ☐ Added Appendix B, which details those countermeasures recommended in the paper that are applicable to the Windows 95/98 environment.

Version 2.0 --
- ☐ Added details regarding the e-mail security patch that Microsoft released for Outlook 98 and Outlook 2000 in response to the ILOVEYOU worm and similar threats.
- ☐ Pointed out that if one wishes to disable cscript.exe or wscript.exe by changing their names it is best to do so from the command prompt.

Version 2.1
- ☐ Added recommendation to enable the display of file extensions.

Version 2.2
- ☐ Added details concerning a feature of Office 2000 SR-1, which allows the definition of file types that cannot be directly executed from a mail message but must instead be saved to the file system prior to execution. Of note is that this feature works for users who utilize .pst files while similar countermeasures do not.

Version 2.3
- ☐ Added detail concerning a patch for protecting against malicious code using CDO in Outlook 98/2000.
- ☐ Updated URLs to reflect the current location of referenced material.

Version 2.4
- ☐ Added a recommendation to delete a registry key so that .pif file extensions will be displayed.
- ☐ Updated a URL to reflect a change in the location of referenced material.

Version 2.41
- ☐ Updated recommendations to include one additional security setting available under IE 5.5.

Version 2.42
- ☐ Added the warnings and trademark pages.

Version 2.5
- ☐ Expanded the list of <u>file extensions</u> that should always be displayed.
- ☐ Updated information about the <u>e-mail security patch</u> to include information about a recent revision to the patch.

Version 2.6
- ☐ Updated some URLs.

Version 3.0
- ☐ Incorporated major changes to reflect the latest releases of Office 2000 and Office XP and to cover the Windows 2000 and Windows XP operating systems.
- ☐ Deleted a variety of out-of-date information about deprecated security patches and operating systems.

Version 3.1
- ☐ Added a recommendation to use the "ReadAsPlain" option. This recommendation was included in the client chapter of NSA's Exchange 2000 guidance but was inadvertently left out of this guide.
- ☐ Updated the list of Internet Explorer restricted zone settings to cover later releases of the product including Internet Explorer 6.0 with service pack 2.
- ☐ Expanded the document to include Outlook 2003 and Outlook Express 6.0 with Service Pack 2.
- ☐ Add Addendum A which identifies the file types that can be used as a basis for a creation of a black list of blocked files.